a

MYSTERY MOUNTAIN LODGE
Balance Sheet
December 31, 1996

Assets							Liabilities & S...						
							Liabilities:						

b

Description of transactions:

(a)

NAME _____ DATE _____

SECTION _____

	Assets			=	Liabilities		+	Owners' Equity
	Cash	Land	Building	Office Equipment	Notes Payable	Accounts Payable		Capital Stock
December 31 balances	$ 37000	$ 95000	$125000	$ 51250	$ 80000	$ 28250		$200000
(1)	+25000							+25000
Balances	62000	95000	125000	51250	80000	28250		225000
(2)	-22500	+35000	+55000		+67500			
Balances	39500	130000	180000	51250	147500	28250		225000
(3)				+8500	+8500			
Balances	39500	130000	180000	59750	156000	28250		225000
(4)	+10000				+10000			
Balances	49500	130000	180000	59750	166000	28250		225000
(5)	-28250					-28250		
Balances	21250	130000	180000	59750	166000	0		225000

391,000

391,000

	Assets			=	Liabilities		+	Owners' Equity
	Cash	Accounts Receivable +	Trucks +	Office Equipment +	Notes Payable =	Accounts Payable +		Capital Stock
December 31 balances	$ 9500	$ 8900	$ 58000	$ 3800	$ 20000	$ 5200		$ 55000
(1)	−2700			+2700				
Balances	−10800 +1000	8900 −4000	58000	6500	20000	5200		55000
(2)								
Balances	10800 −3200	34900	58000	6500	20000	5200 −3200		55000
(3)								
Balances	7600 +10000	34900	58000	6500	20000 +100000	2000		55000
(4)								
Balances	17600 −15000	34900	58000 +30500	6500	30000 +15500	2000		55000
(5)								
Balances	2600 20000	34900	88500	6500	45500	2000		55000 20000
(6)								
Balances	22600	4900	88500	6500	45500	2600		75000
	122500	122500				45500 2000 54000 06500		

a

¡HERE COME THE CLOWNS!

Assets

b

a

Assets					

b

a

THE JULIAN BAKERY
Balance Sheet
August 1, 19_94_

Assets			Liabilities & Stockholders' Equity		
Cash	$ 3 69 40		Liabilities:		3 2
Building	84000		Capital Stock		75000
Accounts Receivable	11260		Income taxes payable		8900
Equipment & Fixtures	44500		Notes Payable		74900
Land	67000		Retained Earnings		45700
Supplies	7000		Accounts Payable		16200
					100000
			Stockholders' Equity:		
			Capital Stock .. 75,000		
			Retained Earning 45,700		220700
b Cash	14490		Capital Stock		100000
Building	84000		Income taxes payable		8900
Accounts Receivable	11260		Notes Payable		74900
Equipment & Fixtures	51700		Retain Earnings		45700
Land	67000		Accts Payable		7200
Supplies	8250				

```
      6
    15,740
   -  1 250
    14,490     44,500
            +  7,200
              51 700
```

236700

c Julian Bakery is in a stronger position because stock is up so they are producing more cash and being able to pay off more bills.

a

OLD TOWN PLAYHOUSE				
Balance Sheet				
September 30, 19___				
Assets			**Liabilities & Stockholders' Equity**	
Cash	$		Liabilities:	
Accounts receivable				

b (1)

a

Assets					Liabilities & Owner's Equity				
					Liabilities:				

b (1)

a

General Journal

			LP		Page 1
1996					
April	1	Accounts Payable	5000		
		Cash			5000
			5000		
April	3	Equipment	5900		
		Cash			5900
April	5				
April	10	Cash	1954		
		Equipment			1954
April	12	Cash	200000		
		Capital Stock			200000
April	15	Land	170000		
		Building	365000		
		Equipment	95000		
		Cash			150000
		Note Payable			480000

b   TKO's assets increased however

_____

_____

_____

_____

a

General Journal

				LP		Page 1
19__						
Sept	1	Cash			50000	
		Capital Stock				50000
	10	Land			106000	
		Building			76400	
		Cash				36500
		Notes Payable				145900
	15	Office Equipment			4680	
		Cash				4680
	19	Office Equipment			3960	
		Cash				720
		Acct. Payable				3240
	20	Office Equipment			140	
		Note Payable				140
	28	Acct Payable			1080	
		Cash				1080
	30	Cash			140	
		Acct. Receivable				140

b

_____

_____

_____

_____

_____

a   **Analysis of transactions:**

   (1) (a)

b	General Journal				
		LP			Page 1
19___					
July	2				

a

ENVIRONMENTAL SERVICES, INC.
Trial Balance
November 30, 19___

Cash	$	17650
Notes receivable		

b

ENVIRONMENTAL SERVICES, INC.
Balance Sheet
November 30, 19___

Assets			Liabilities & Stockholders' Equity	
Cash	$	17650	Liabilities:	

c

a **Cash** **Account No. 1**

Date	Explanation	Ref	Debit	Credit	Balance
19__					
July 1			130000		130000
3				30850	99150
17				630	98520
22				3955	

Office Supplies **Account No. 9**

Date	Explanation	Ref	Debit	Credit	Balance
19__					
7			1260		

Land **Account No. 20**

Date	Explanation	Ref	Debit	Credit	Balance
19__					
3			48400		

Tennis Courts **Account No. 22**

Date	Explanation	Ref	Debit	Credit	Balance
19__					
3			75000		

Tennis Equipment **Account No. 25**

Date	Explanation	Ref	Debit	Credit	Balance
19__					
6			4680		
12				725	

35435

Notes Payable — Account No. 30

Date	Explanation	Ref	Debit	Credit	Balance
19__					
3				92550	

Accounts Payable — Account No. 31

Date	Explanation	Ref	Debit	Credit	Balance
19__					
6				4680	
7				1260	
12			725		
17			630		
22			3955		

Capital Stock — Account No. 50

Date	Explanation	Ref	Debit	Credit	Balance
19__					
1			130000	130000	

b

WINNERS' TENNIS COLLEGE
Trial Balance
July 31, 19__

	Debit	Credit
Cash	$ 94565	
Office supplies	1260	
Land	48400	
Tennis courts	75000	
Tennis equipment	3955	
Notes Payable		92550
Acct. Payable		630
Capital Stock		130000
	223180	223180

NAME ________________________

SECTION ____________ DATE ____________

c

WINNERS' TENNIS COLLEGE

Balance Sheet

July 31, 19__

Assets		Liabilities & Stockholders' Equity		
Cash	94565	Liabilities:		
Office Supplies	1260	Notes Payable		92550
Land	48400	Acct. Payable		630
Tennis Courts	75000			93180
Tennis Equip.	3955			
		Capital Stock	130,000	130000
	223180			223180

5310 5940

a

Page 1

General Journal

LP

19___					

b

Cash					Account No. 10
Date	Explanation	Ref	Debit	Credit	Balance
19___					

Accounts Receivable					Account No. 11
Date	Explanation	Ref	Debit	Credit	Balance
19___					

Land					Account No. 16
Date	Explanation	Ref	Debit	Credit	Balance
19___					

Buildings					Account No. 17
Date	Explanation	Ref	Debit	Credit	Balance
19___					

Office Equipment — Account No. 20

Date	Explanation	Ref	Debit	Credit	Balance
19__					

Buses — Account No. 22

Date	Explanation	Ref	Debit	Credit	Balance
19__					

Notes Payable — Account No. 31

Date	Explanation	Ref	Debit	Credit	Balance
19__					

Accounts Payable — Account No. 32

Date	Explanation	Ref	Debit	Credit	Balance
19__					

Capital Stock — Account No. 50

Date	Explanation	Ref	Debit	Credit	Balance
19__					

c

WALNUT CREEK TRANSPORTATION SERVICES		
Trial Balance		
July 31, 19___		
Cash	$	
Accounts receivable		
Land		
Buildings		
Office Equipment		
Buses		

d

a

General Journal

		LP		Page 1

19___

b

		Cash			Account No. 1
Date	**Explanation**	**Ref**	**Debit**	**Credit**	**Balance**
19___					

		Notes Receivable			Account No. 5
Date	**Explanation**	**Ref**	**Debit**	**Credit**	**Balance**
19___					

		Land			Account No. 21
Date	**Explanation**	**Ref**	**Debit**	**Credit**	**Balance**
19___					

		Building			Account No. 23
Date	**Explanation**	**Ref**	**Debit**	**Credit**	**Balance**
19___					

Office Equipment					Account No. 25
Date	Explanation	Ref	Debit	Credit	Balance
19__					

Notes Payable					Account No. 31
Date	Explanation	Ref	Debit	Credit	Balance
19__					

Accounts Payable					Account No. 32
Date	Explanation	Ref	Debit	Credit	Balance
19__					

Capital Stock					Account No. 51
Date	Explanation	Ref	Debit	Credit	Balance
19__					

c	**RYAN PROPERTY MANAGEMENT**						
	Trial Balance						
	November 30, 19___						
Cash		$					
Notes receivable							
Land							
Building							

d

a Page 1

General Journal

LP

19__					
Feb					
1	Cash	+	350000		
	Capital Stock	+			350000
3	Land	+	120000		
	Building	+	95000		
	Equipment	+	110000		
	Cash	−			200000
	Note Payable	+			125000
	Transmitter				
5	Equipment	+	225000		
	Cash	−			75000
	Note Payable	+			150000
9	Film Library	+	50000		
	Cash	−			15000
	Accts Payable	+			35000
12	Supplies	+	3190		
	Cash	−			3190
15	Note Payable	+	12500		
	Cash	−			12500
25	Accts Receivable	+	8900		
	Film Library	−			8900

b

Date	Explanation	Ref	Debit	Credit	Balance
					Cash — Account No. 11
19__			350000		
Feb 1					
Feb 3				200000	150000
5				75000	325000
9				15000	375000
12				3190	378190
15				12500	390000
15				305690	

Accounts Receivable — Account No. 15

Date	Explanation	Ref	Debit	Credit	Balance
19__					
25			8900		

Supplies — Account No. 19

Date	Explanation	Ref	Debit	Credit	Balance
19__					
12			3190		

Land — Account No. 21

Date	Explanation	Ref	Debit	Credit	Balance
19__					
3			120000		

Building					Account No. 22
Date	Explanation	Ref	Debit	Credit	Balance
19___					
3			95000		

Transmitter					Account No. 23
Date	Explanation	Ref	Debit	Credit	Balance
19___					
5			255000		

Telecasting Equipment					Account No. 24
Date	Explanation	Ref	Debit	Credit	Balance
19___					
3			110000		

Film Library					Account No. 25
Date	Explanation	Ref	Debit	Credit	Balance
19___					
9			50000		
25				8900	

Notes Payable					Account No. 31
Date	Explanation	Ref	Debit	Credit	Balance
19___					
3				125000	
5				150000	
15			12500	278000	
				− 12500	
				262500	

349 8
3810 1000
−305,690
44,310   305,690

					Account No. 32
Date	**Explanation**	**Ref**	**Debit**	**Credit**	**Balance**

19___					
9				35000	

Accounts Payable

					Account No. 51
Date	**Explanation**	**Ref**	**Debit**	**Credit**	**Balance**

19___					
1				350000	

Capital Stock

c

COMMUNITY TV, INC.
Trial Balance
February 28, 19___

	Debit	Credit
Cash	44310	
Accounts receivable	8900	
Supplies	3190	
Land	120000	
Building	95000	
Transmitter	255000	
Telecasting equipment	110000	
Film library	41100	
Notes payable		262500
Accounts payable		35000
Capital stock		350000

d

COMMUNITY TV, INC.
Balance Sheet
February 28, 19___

Assets			Liabilities & Stockholders' Equity	
Cash	$	44310	Liabilities:	
Accounts receivable		8900	Notes Payable	$262500
Supplies		3190	Accts. Payable	35000
Land	120000			297500
Building	95000		Capital Stock 350,000	350000
Transmitter	225000			
Tele.	110000			647500
Film Library	91100			
	647500			

e   No, the corporation does not have enough money.

a   Page 1

General Journal

				LP		
1995						
Mar	1	Cash			48000	
		Accounts Receivable			8600	

b

Cash					Account No. 1
Date	Explanation	Ref	Debit	Credit	Balance
1995					

Accounts Receivable					Account No. 5
Date	Explanation	Ref	Debit	Credit	Balance
1995					

Supplies					Account No. 8
Date	Explanation	Ref	Debit	Credit	Balance
1995					

Spare Parts					Account No. 15
Date	Explanation	Ref	Debit	Credit	Balance
1995					

Buildings					Account No. 20
Date	Explanation	Ref	Debit	Credit	Balance
1995					

Equipment & Rolling Stock — Account No. 22

Date	Explanation	Ref	Debit	Credit	Balance
1995					

Roadbed, Track, & Ties — Account No. 24

Date	Explanation	Ref	Debit	Credit	Balance
1995					

Right-of-Way — Account No. 26

Date	Explanation	Ref	Debit	Credit	Balance
1995					

Notes Payable — Account No. 30

Date	Explanation	Ref	Debit	Credit	Balance
1995					

Accounts Payable — Account No. 32

Date	Explanation	Ref	Debit	Credit	Balance
1995					

| | Capital Stock | | | | Account No. 50 |
Date	Explanation	Ref	Debit	Credit	Balance
1995					

c

LITTLE BEAR RAILROAD, INC.
Trial Balance
March 15, 1995

Cash		
Accounts receivable		
Supplies		
Spare parts		
Buildings		
Equipment & rolling stock		
Roadbed, track, & ties		
Right-of-way		
Notes payable		
Accounts payable		
Capital stock		

d	LITTLE BEAR RAILROAD, INC.						
	Balance Sheet						
	March 15, 1995						
Assets				**Liabilities & Stockholders' Equity**			
				Liabilities:			

Note to financial statements:

e

a

General Journal

LP

a

General Journal

LP

b

_____

a   **Analysis of transactions:**

    (1) *(a)* Rent is an operating expense. Expenses are recorded by debits. Debit Rent Expense, $4,400.

          (b) The asset Cash was decreased. Decreases in assets are recorded by credits. Credit Cash, $4,400.

    (2) *(a)*

b

Aug	1													

a   **Analysis of transactions:**

    (1) *(a)* **Rent is an operating expense. Expenses are recorded by debits. Debit Rent Expense, $2,400.**

          (b) **The asset Cash was decreased. Decreases in assets are recorded by credits. Credit Cash, $2,400.**

    (2) *(a)*

b						
July	1					

a   **General Journal**

Cambell Crop Dusting   **LP**   **Page 1**

1996				
June	1	Cash	60000	
		Capital Stock		60000
June	2	Aircraft	220000	
		Cash		40000
		Note Payable		180000
June	4	Rent Expense	2500	
		Cash		2500
June	15	Acct. Receivable	8320	
		Crop Dusting Revenue		8320
June	15	Salary Expense	5880	
		Cash		5880
June	18	Maintenance Expense	1890	
		Cash		1890
June	25	Cash	4910	
		Acct. Receivable		4910
June	30	Acct. Receivable	16450	
		Crop Dusting Revenue		16450
June	30	Salary Expense	6000	
		Cash		6000
June	30	Fuel Expense	2510	
		Accounts Payable		2510
June	30	Dividends	2000	
		Dividends Payable		2000

Your not paymable until the frre
so you put how much you of (debt)
and put a dividend payable because you
will later pay that.

Antoinette Wisniewski

Antoinette Wisniewski

	Cash				Account No. 1
Date	Explanation	Ref	Debit	Credit	Balance

	Accounts Receivable				Account No. 5
Date	Explanation	Ref	Debit	Credit	Balance

	Aircraft				Account No. 15
Date	Explanation	Ref	Debit	Credit	Balance

	Notes Payable				Account No. 31
Date	Explanation	Ref	Debit	Credit	Balance

	Accounts Payable				Account No. 32
Date	Explanation	Ref	Debit	Credit	Balance

Dividends Payable — Account No. 35

Date	Explanation	Ref	Debit	Credit	Balance

Capital Stock — Account No. 40

Date	Explanation	Ref	Debit	Credit	Balance

Retained Earnings — Account No. 41

Date	Explanation	Ref	Debit	Credit	Balance

Dividends — Account No. 45

Date	Explanation	Ref	Debit	Credit	Balance

Crop Dusting Revenue — Account No. 51

Date	Explanation	Ref	Debit	Credit	Balance

Maintenance Expense — Account No. 61

Date	Explanation	Ref	Debit	Credit	Balance

	Fuel Expense				Account No. 62
Date	Explanation	Ref	Debit	Credit	Balance

	Salaries Expense				Account No. 63
Date	Explanation	Ref	Debit	Credit	Balance

	Rent Expense				Account No. 64
Date	Explanation	Ref	Debit	Credit	Balance

CAMPBELL CROP DUSTING

Trial Balance

June 30, 1996

Cash	$	
Accounts receivable		
Aircraft		
Notes payable		
Accounts payable		
Dividends payable		
Capital stock		
Retained earnings		
Dividends		
Crop dusting revenue		
Maintenance expense		
Fuel expense		
Salaries expense		
Rent expense		

d

Total assets:

Total liabilities:

Total stockholders' equity:

↓ on exam

a

ENVIRONMENTAL SOLUTIONS, INC.
Income Statement
For the Year Ended December 31, 1996

Revenue: Consulting Fees Earned		487200
Expenses:		
Advertising Exp.	31500	
Insurance Exp.	38720	
Utilites Exp.	15040	
Salaries Exp	245280	
Depreciation Exp: Building	4200	
Depreciation Exp: Office Equipment	3360	338100
Income before income taxes		149100
Income taxes expense		59640
Net Income		89460

p. 115

ENVIRONMENTAL SOLUTIONS, INC.
Statement of Retained Earnings
For the Year Ended December 31, 1996

Retained earnings, Jan. 1, 1996		181300
Add: Net Income for Dec.	89460	89460
Subtotal	89460	270760
Less: Dividends	70000	70000
		200760
Retained Earings, Dec 30 ↑		

b

↓ p. 115

ENVIRONMENTAL SOLUTIONS, INC.
Balance Sheet
December 31, 1996

Assets

Cash		57690
Note Receivable		12740
Acct. Receivable		65090
Land		196000
Building	126,000	
Less: Acc. depreciation	33,600	92400
Office Equipment	33,600	
Less: Acc depreciation	13,440	20160
Total assets		444080

Liabilities & Stockholders' Equity

Liabilities:

Notes Payable		112000
Acct. Payable		22680
Income taxes Payable		59640
Total liabilities		194320
Stockholders' equity:		
Capital stock	49000	249760
Retained earnings		444080
Total Stockholders' equity	200760	
Total Liab. & stockholders' equity		

parts c and d

c   **Income tax rate used was**

$$\frac{\text{Income tax expense} \quad 49640}{\text{Income before taxes} \quad 59100} = 40\%$$

d   **Estimated useful life of building is**

$124,000 - cost of building

$33,600 - Depreciation

Circle the ones you are closing out!

a

		General Journal (Closing Entries)	LP		
Dec	31	~~Consulting fees earned~~			~~487200~~
		~~Consulting fees earned~~		487200	
		~~Income Summary~~			487200
		Income Summary		397740	
		⟨ Adv. Exp.			31500
		Insurance Exp			
		Utilities Exp			
		Salaries Exp.			
		Dep: Building			
		Dep: Off. Eq.			
		Income tax exp. ⟩			
		Income Summary		89460	
		Retained Earnings			89460
		Retained Earnings		70000	
		Div.			70000

b

Income Summary

① 487200	487200
② 397740	89460

89460
+70000
159460
15

Retained Earnings

③ 89460	181300 Adjusted Trial Balance (CR)
④ 70000	270760 (CR)
	200760 (CR)

a

URSUS ENTERPRISES, INC.
Income Statement
For the Year Ended December 31, 1996

Revenue:

URSUS ENTERPRISES, INC.
Statement of Retained Earnings
For the Year Ended December 31, 1996

Retained earnings, January 1, 1996

---

b

URSUS ENTERPRISES, INC.
Balance Sheet
December 31, 1996

Assets

Liabilities & Stockholders' Equity

Liabilities:

parts c and d

c

d

a   *General Journal*

LP

Dec	31											

b   **Following Year—Entry to close Income Summary account.**

a   **The errors Webb made are:**

   (1)

General Journal
a **(Adjusting Entries)**

Mar	31					

e **(Closing Entries)**

Mar	31					

c

HEMPSTEAD REALTY
Adjusted Trial Balance
March 31, 19___

d

HEMPSTEAD REALTY
Income Statement
For the Month Ended March 31, 19___

Revenue:

d (continued)

HEMPSTEAD REALTY
Statement of Retained Earnings
For the Month Ended March 31, 19___

Retained earnings, March 1, 19___

Add:

e

HEMPSTEAD REALTY
Balance Sheet
March 31, 19___

Assets

Liabilities & Stockholders' Equity

Liabilities:

f

HEMPSTEAD REALTY
After-Closing Trial Balance
March 31, 19___

a	*General Journal*		LP									Page 1					
19___																	
May	1																

General Journal

LP   Page 2

19___

General Journal

d   **(Adjusting Entries)**   *LP*   Page 3

h   **(Closing Entries)**

b, d, g

Cash — Account No. 10

Date	Explanation	Ref	Debit	Credit	Balance

Accounts Receivable — Account No. 13

Date	Explanation	Ref	Debit	Credit	Balance

Medical Instruments — Account No. 20

Date	Explanation	Ref	Debit	Credit	Balance

Accumulated Depreciation: Medical Instruments — Account No. 21

Date	Explanation	Ref	Debit	Credit	Balance

Office Equipment — Account No. 22

Date	Explanation	Ref	Debit	Credit	Balance

Accumulated Depreciation: Office Equipment					**Account No. 23**
Date	**Explanation**	**Ref**	**Debit**	**Credit**	**Balance**

Notes Payable					**Account No. 30**
Date	**Explanation**	**Ref**	**Debit**	**Credit**	**Balance**

Accounts Payable					**Account No. 31**
Date	**Explanation**	**Ref**	**Debit**	**Credit**	**Balance**

Dividends Payable					**Account No. 32**
Date	**Explanation**	**Ref**	**Debit**	**Credit**	**Balance**

Income Taxes Payable					**Account No. 33**
Date	**Explanation**	**Ref**	**Debit**	**Credit**	**Balance**

Capital Stock					**Account No. 40**
Date	**Explanation**	**Ref**	**Debit**	**Credit**	**Balance**

Retained Earnings — Account No. 45

Date	Explanation	Ref	Debit	Credit	Balance

Dividends — Account No. 47

Date	Explanation	Ref	Debit	Credit	Balance

Income Summary — Account No. 49

Date	Explanation	Ref	Debit	Credit	Balance

Fees Earned — Account No. 50

Date	Explanation	Ref	Debit	Credit	Balance

Medical Supplies Expense — Account No. 60

Date	Explanation	Ref	Debit	Credit	Balance

	Rent Expense				Account No. 61
Date	Explanation	Ref	Debit	Credit	Balance

	Salaries Expense				Account No. 62
Date	Explanation	Ref	Debit	Credit	Balance

	Utilities Expense				Account No. 63
Date	Explanation	Ref	Debit	Credit	Balance

	Depreciation Expense: Medical Instruments				Account No. 64
Date	Explanation	Ref	Debit	Credit	Balance

	Depreciation Expense: Office Equipment				Account No. 65
Date	Explanation	Ref	Debit	Credit	Balance

	Income Taxes Expense				Account No. 66
Date	Explanation	Ref	Debit	Credit	Balance

c

AVERY SLOAN, M.D., INCORPORATED
Trial Balance
May 31, 19___

Cash		
Accounts receivable		
Medical instruments		
Office equipment		
Notes payable		
Accounts payable		
Dividends payable		
Capital stock		
Dividends		
Fees earned		
Medical supplies expense		
Rent expense		
Salaries expense		
Utilities expense		

f

AVERY SLOAN, M.D., INCORPORATED
Adjusted Trial Balance
May 31, 19___

Cash		
Accounts receivable		
Medical instruments		
Accumulated depreciation: medical instruments		
Office equipment		
Accumulated depreciation: office equipment		
Notes payable		
Accounts payable		
Dividends payable		

g

AVERY SLOAN, M.D., INCORPORATED
Income Statement
For the Month Ended May 31, 19___

Revenue:

AVERY SLOAN, M.D., INCORPORATED
Statement of Retained Earnings
For the Month Ended May 31, 19___

Retained earnings, May 1, 19___

AVERY SLOAN, M.D., INCORPORATED
Balance Sheet
May 31, 19___

Assets

Liabilities & Stockholders' Equity

Liabilities:

AVERY SLOAN, M.D., INCORPORATED After-Closing Trial Balance May 31, 19___		
Cash		
Accounts receivable		
Medical instruments		
Accumulated depreciation: medical instruments		
Office equipment		
Accumulated depreciation: office equipment		
Notes payable		

General Journal

a		LP									Page 1
19___											

General Journal

LP   Page 2

19____

Adjusting Entries

d

19____

e

h

General Journal

LP   Page 3

Closing Entries

19___

b, d, e, h   Cash   Account No. 1

Date	Explanation	Ref	Debit	Credit	Balance
19__					

Accounts Receivable   Account No. 3

Date	Explanation	Ref	Debit	Credit	Balance
19__					

Land   Account No. 11

Date	Explanation	Ref	Debit	Credit	Balance
19__					

Building   Account No. 12

Date	Explanation	Ref	Debit	Credit	Balance
19__					

Accumulated Depreciation: Building   Account No. 13

Date	Explanation	Ref	Debit	Credit	Balance
19__					

		Trucks			Account No. 15	
Date	Explanation	Ref	Debit	Credit	Balance	
19__						

		Accumulated Depreciation: Trucks			Account No. 16	
Date	Explanation	Ref	Debit	Credit	Balance	
19__						

		Office Equipment			Account No. 18	
Date	Explanation	Ref	Debit	Credit	Balance	
19__						

		Accumulated Depreciation: Office Equipment			Account No. 19	
Date	Explanation	Ref	Debit	Credit	Balance	
19__						

		Notes Payable			Account No. 30	
Date	Explanation	Ref	Debit	Credit	Balance	
19__						

Accounts Payable — Account No. 31

Date	Explanation	Ref	Debit	Credit	Balance
19___					

Dividends Payable — Account No. 32

Date	Explanation	Ref	Debit	Credit	Balance
19___					

Income Taxes Payable — Account No. 33

Date	Explanation	Ref	Debit	Credit	Balance
19___					

Capital Stock — Account No. 40

Date	Explanation	Ref	Debit	Credit	Balance
19___					

Retained Earnings — Account No. 41

Date	Explanation	Ref	Debit	Credit	Balance
19___					

Dividends — Account No. 45

Date	Explanation	Ref	Debit	Credit	Balance
19___					

Income Summary   Account No. 50

Date	Explanation	Ref	Debit	Credit	Balance
19__					

Moving Service Revenue   Account No. 60

Date	Explanation	Ref	Debit	Credit	Balance
19__					

Salaries Expense   Account No. 70

Date	Explanation	Ref	Debit	Credit	Balance
19__					

Gasoline Expense   Account No. 71

Date	Explanation	Ref	Debit	Credit	Balance
19__					

Repairs & Maintenance Expense   Account No. 72

Date	Explanation	Ref	Debit	Credit	Balance
19__					

Interest Expense					Account No. 73
Date	Explanation	Ref	Debit	Credit	Balance
19___					

Depreciation Expense: Building					Account No. 74
Date	Explanation	Ref	Debit	Credit	Balance
19___					

Depreciation Expense: Trucks					Account No. 75
Date	Explanation	Ref	Debit	Credit	Balance
19___					

Depreciation Expense: Office Equipment					Account No. 76
Date	Explanation	Ref	Debit	Credit	Balance
19___					

Income Taxes Expense					Account No. 77
Date	Explanation	Ref	Debit	Credit	Balance
19___					

c

GLOBAL TRANSPORT, INC.
Trial Balance
November 30, 19___

Cash		
Accounts receivable		
Land		
Building		
Trucks		
Office equipment		
Notes payable		
Accounts payable		
Dividends payable		
Capital stock		
Dividends		
Moving service revenue		
Salaries expense		
Gasoline expense		
Repairs & maintenance expense		
Interest expense		

f

GLOBAL TRANSPORT, INC.
Adjusted Trial Balance
November 30, 19___

Cash		
Accounts receivable		
Land		
Building		
Accumulated depreciation: building		
Trucks		
Accumulated depreciation: trucks		
Office equipment		
Accumulated depreciation: office equipment		
Notes payable		
Accounts payable		
Dividends payable		

g

GLOBAL TRANSPORT, INC.
Income Statement
For the Month Ended November 30, 19___

GLOBAL TRANSPORT, INC.
Statement of Retained Earnings
For the Month Ended November 30, 19___

Retained earnings, November 1, 19___

GLOBAL TRANSPORT, INC.
Balance Sheet
November 30, 19___

Assets

Liabilities & Stockholders' Equity

Liabilities:

i	GLOBAL TRANSPORT, INC.		
	After-Closing Trial Balance		
	November 30, 19___		
Cash			
Accounts receivable			
Land			
Building			
Accumulated depreciation: building			
Trucks			
Accumulated depreciation: trucks			
Office equipment			
Accumulated depreciation: office equipment			
Notes payable			

General Journal
(Adjusting Entries)

19__				
Dec 31	Salary Exp. (a)		7900	
	Salaries Payable			7900
31	Rent Receivable (b)		11075	
	Rent Revenue			11075
31	Unearned Rental Revenue (c)		6400	
	Rental Revenue			6400
31	Limousine Rental Exp. (d)		1560	
	Rent Payable			1560
31	Interest Exp.	+	250	
	Interest Payable (e)	+		250
31	Dep. Exp.: Building (f)	+	58500	
	Acc Dep.: Building	+		58500
	No entry (g)			
31	Insurance Exp.		2400	
	Unexpired Insurance			2400
	Income Taxes Exp.	+	7200	
	Income Taxes Payable	+		7200

1560

3200
x 2
6400

a   *General Journal*

5 | 17,000 28
12)3420

May	31				
		Dep. Exp. : Office Equipment.	+	285	
		Acc. Dep. : Office Equipment	+		285
		17,000 × 1/5 × 1/12			
		Unearned Retainer Fees	−	6400	
		Fees Earned	+		6400
		Salaries Exp.		1665	
		Salaries Payable			1665
		Rent Expense		1800	
		Prepaid Rent			1800
		(5,400 × 3 = 1800)			
		Fees Receivable	+	2900	
		Fees Earned	+		2900
		Office Supplies Exp.	+	350	
		Office Supplies.	−		350
		($1,050 − $700 = $350)			
				400	
		Insurance Exp.			400
		Unexpired Insurance			
		($2,400 ÷ 6 mos. = $400)			
		Income Taxes Exp.		2200	
		Income Taxes payable			2200

17|4
7)13,030

b

Computation of net income to be reported in income
statement for May:

   Fees earned (per trial balance)

   Add:

a

General Journal
(Adjusting Entries)

1996

Apr

General Journal
(Adjusting Entries)

1996				
b	Computation of the amount of net income to be reported in the income statement for April:			
	Legal fees earned (per trial balance)			
	Add:			

a *(1)* Age of the catamaran in months

b	General Journal		LP	
	Adjusting Entries			
19___	(1)			
June 30				

General Journal
(Adjusting Entries)

1996		*(a)*					
Dec	31						

General Journal
(Closing Entries)

1996					
Dec	31				

b

ISLAND HOPPER

Income Statement

For the Month Ended June 30, 1996

Revenue:

ISLAND HOPPER

Statement of Retained Earnings

For the Month Ended June 30, 1996

Retained earnings, May 31, 1996

Add:

ISLAND HOPPER
Balance Sheet
June 30, 1996

Assets

Liabilities & Stockholders' Equity

Liabilities:

Stockholders' equity:

c   **Note 1:**

d

General Journal
(Adjusting Entries)

1996					
June	30				

d (continued)

General Journal
(Closing Entries)

1996				
June	30			

a	General Journal			
		LP		Page 1
19__				
Sept 1				

General Journal

LP   Page 2

19____

(Use General Journal pages 3 and 4, provided at the
end of the working papers for this problem, for
recording adjusting and closing entries.)

b

| | | | | | Cash | | | | | Account No. 1 |
Date		Explanation		Ref		Debit		Credit		Balance

| | | | | | Accounts Receivable | | | | | Account No. 4 |
Date		Explanation		Ref		Debit		Credit		Balance

| | | | | | Prepaid Rent | | | | | Account No. 6 |
Date		Explanation		Ref		Debit		Credit		Balance

| | | | | | Unexpired Insurance | | | | | Account No. 7 |
Date		Explanation		Ref		Debit		Credit		Balance

Office Supplies — Account No. 8

Date	Explanation	Ref	Debit	Credit	Balance

Rental Equipment — Account No. 10

Date	Explanation	Ref	Debit	Credit	Balance

Accumulated Depreciation: Rental Equipment — Account No. 12

Date	Explanation	Ref	Debit	Credit	Balance

Notes Payable — Account No. 20

Date	Explanation	Ref	Debit	Credit	Balance

			Accounts Payable				Account No. 22
Date		Explanation	Ref	Debit		Credit	Balance

			Interest Payable				Account No. 25
Date		Explanation	Ref	Debit		Credit	Balance

			Salaries Payable				Account No. 26
Date		Explanation	Ref	Debit		Credit	Balance

			Dividends Payable				Account No. 27
Date		Explanation	Ref	Debit		Credit	Balance

Unearned Rental Fees   Account No. 28

Date	Explanation	Ref	Debit	Credit	Balance

Income Taxes Payable   Account No. 29

Date	Explanation	Ref	Debit	Credit	Balance

Capital Stock   Account No. 30

Date	Explanation	Ref	Debit	Credit	Balance

Retained Earnings   Account No. 35

Date	Explanation	Ref	Debit	Credit	Balance

Dividends   Account No. 38

Date	Explanation	Ref	Debit	Credit	Balance

Income Summary — Account No. 40

Date	Explanation	Ref	Debit	Credit	Balance

Rental Fees Earned — Account No. 50

Date	Explanation	Ref	Debit	Credit	Balance

Salaries Expense — Account No. 60

Date	Explanation	Ref	Debit	Credit	Balance

Maintenance Expense — Account No. 61

Date	Explanation	Ref	Debit	Credit	Balance

Utilities Expense — Account No. 62

Date	Explanation	Ref	Debit	Credit	Balance

		Rent Expense				Account No. 63
Date	Explanation	Ref	Debit	Credit	Balance

		Office Supplies Expense				Account No. 64
Date	Explanation	Ref	Debit	Credit	Balance

		Depreciation Expense				Account No. 65
Date	Explanation	Ref	Debit	Credit	Balance

		Interest Expense				Account No. 66
Date	Explanation	Ref	Debit	Credit	Balance

		Income Taxes Expense				Account No. 67
Date	Explanation	Ref	Debit	Credit	Balance

d

FRIEND WITH A TRUCK, INC.
Income Statement
For the Month Ended September 30, 19___

Revenue:

FRIEND WITH A TRUCK, INC.
Statement of Retained Earnings
For the Month Ended September 31, 19___

Retained earnings, September 1, 19___		$	–0–

FRIEND WITH A TRUCK, INC.
Balance Sheet
September 30, 19___

Assets

Cash

Accounts receivable

Liabilities & Stockholders' Equity

Liabilities:

Notes payable

e **Notes to the financial statements:**

Note 1—Depreciation policies

f		*General Journal*					
		(Adjusting entries)	**LP**				**Page 3**
19___							
Sept	30						

(Record closing entries on next page.)

General Journal
(Closing entries)   LP   Page 4

19 __				
Sept	30			

FRIEND WITH A TRUCK, INC.

g   *After-Closing Trial Balance*

September 30, 19___

Cash	$	
Accounts receivable		
Prepaid rent		
Unexpired insurance		
Office supplies		
Rental equipment		
Accumulated depreciation: rental equipment		
Notes payable		

a | *General Journal*

LP

1996		
Nov	5	

b

INDIAN LAKE LUMBER CO.
Partial Income Statement
For the Year Ended December 31, 1996

Net sales

c

a	General Journal			
		LP		
19___				
May	10			

Item Mitsui P-500 facsimile

Description Plain paper facsimile

Location 1 in showroom, remainder in warehouse

Primary supplier Mitsui Corporation

Secondary supplier None

Inventory level: Minimum 1 **Maximum** 10

Date	PURCHASED			SOLD			BALANCE		
	Units	Unit Cost	Total	Units	Unit Cost	Total	Units	Unit Cost	Balance

c

a   **Computation of the cost of goods sold:**

a	General Journal							
		LP						
19___								
Jan 2	Cash				40000			

General Journal

LP

a   **Journal of 21st Century:**

		General Journal														
			LP													
a		Journal entries by Texas Wholesale Corp.														
Feb	9															

		General Journal			
				LP	

c

General Journal

		LP		
a	**Entries in accounts of Riviera Fashions:**			
Mar 3	Acct. Receivable		500 00	
	Sales			500 00
	CGS		320 00	
	Inventory			320 00
Mar 5	Acct. Payable		50 00	
	Inventory			50 00
	Inventory		32 00	
Mar 15	CGS			32 00
Mar 15	Acct. Receivable		450 00	
	Sales			450 00
	Caroline's			
Mar 3	Inventory		500 00	
	Acct. Payable			500 00
Mar 5	Sales Return		50 00	
	Acct Receivable			50 00
Mar 13	Accts. Payable		450 00	
	Cash			450 00

General Journal

			LP				

d

Parts a, c, and g; Parts b, d, e, and f are on the following page.

b   *General Journal*

LP

1996

Jan 2

d   Computation of inventory at January 6:

e   Journal entries assuming use of a periodic system:

1996

Jan 2

f   Computation of cost of goods sold:

a

a

___ **a** Paid an invoice in which the supplier had accidentally doubled the price of the merchandise.

___ **b** Paid a supplier for goods that were delivered, but that were never ordered.

___ **c** Purchased merchandise which turned out not to be popular with customers.

___ **d** Several sales invoices were misplaced and the accounts receivable department is therefore unaware of the unrecorded credit sales.

___ **e** Paid a supplier for goods that were never ordered.

___ **f** The purchasing department ordered goods from one supplier when a better price could have been obtained by ordering from another supplier.

___ **g** The cashier conceals the embezzlement of cash by reducing the balance of the Cash account.

___ *a* A salesclerk unknowingly makes a credit sale to a customer whose account has already reached the customer's prearranged credit limit.

___ *b* The cashier of a business conceals a theft of cash by adjusting the balance of the Cash account in the company's computer-based accounting records.

___ *c* Certain merchandise proves to be so unpopular with customers that it cannot be sold except at a price well below its original cost.

___ *d* A salesclerk rings up a sale at an incorrect price.

___ *e* A salesclerk uses a point-of-sale terminal to improperly reduce the balance of a friend's account in the company's accounts receivable records.

___ *f* One of the salesclerks is quite lazy and leaves most of the work of serving customers to the other salesclerks in the department.

___ *g* A shoplifter steals merchandise while the salesclerk is busy with another customer.

a

a

a

a

		(Dollars in Millions)
a	**Current assets:**	
	Cash	

b **(1)** **Current ratio:**

c

		(Dollars in Thousands)

a   *(1)*   **Quick assets:**

(2)   **Current assets:**

(3)   **Current liabilities:**

b   *(1)*   **Quick ratio:**

(2)   **Current ratio:**

(3)   **Working capital:**

(4)   **Debt ratio:**

c

			$						
a	**Current assets:**								
	Cash		$						
	Marketable securities								

b _____

a   (1)

WESTPORT DEPARTMENT STORE

Balance Sheet

December 31, 1996

(Dollars in Thousands)

Assets

Current assets $

Plant and equipment

Supporting computations:

(1)   Other assets:

(2)   Stockholders' equity:

a (2)

WESTPORT DEPARTMENT STORE
Income Statement
For the Year Ended December 31, 1996

(Dollars in Thousands)

Net sales		$
Less:		

Supporting computations:

(1) Gross profit:

(In Thousands)

b (1) Current ratio:

c (1) Gross profit rate:

(2) Return on total assets:

a

(Dollars in Millions)

	1988	1989	1990	1991	1992
	$	$	$	$	$
	$	$	$	$	$

(1) Percentage changes in net sales (1989–1992):

Net sales

Less net sales in the prior year

Change in net sales

Percentage change

(2) Gross profit rates (1989–1992):

(Dollars in Thousands)

a Current ratio:
  (1) Beginning of year

b Working capital:
  (1) Beginning of year

d *(1)* Return on average total assets:

c and **e**

a		Gibson Greetings Inc.		American Greetings	
(1) Current ratio:					
($			to 1		
($					to 1
(2) Working capital (dollar amounts in thousands):					
		$			
				$	
(3) Return on average total assets:					
			%		
					%
(4) Return on average total stockholders' equity:			%		
					%

b _____

_____

_____

_____

_____

_____

_____

_____

_____

_____

_____

	(Dollars in Millions)	
	1992	**1991**
a **(1)**		
	to 1	
		to 1
(2) Current ratio:		
(3) Working capital:		

Part b appears on the following page.

c Percentage changes from 1991:

In net sales [($

In net income [($

d **(1)** Gross profit rate:		
	%	
		%
(2) Net income as a percentage of sales:		
	%	
		%
(3) Return on average assets:		
	%	
		%
(4) Return on average assets:		
	%	
		%

Part e appears on the following page.

b

a

SHOWTIME VIDEO
Statement of Cash Flows
For the Year Ended December 31, 1996

Cash flows from operating activities:		
	$	
		$

b

a

BOSTON CELTICS LIMITED PARTNERSHIP
Statement of Cash Flows
For the Year ended June 30, 1989

	(Dollars in Thousands)
Cash flows from operating activities:	
Regular season receipts:	
	$

b

Parts a, c, e, and f appear on the following page.

b **(1)** **Current ratio:**

   Current assets:

      Cash $

(2) **Quick ratio:**

   Quick assets:

(3) **Working capital:**

(4) **Debt ratio:**

d **(1)** **Return on assets:**

(2) **Return on equity:**

a

a

	Dollars in Millions For the Years Ended	
	Jan. 30, 1993	Feb. 1, 1992
a (1) Current ratio:		
($ ÷ $)	to 1	
($ ÷ $)		to 1
(2) Quick ratio:		

Comprehensive Problem 4
Toys "R" Us: Part III

	Dollars in Millions For the Years Ended	
	Jan. 30, 1993	Feb. 1, 1992
a (1) **Percentage change in net sales:**		
Net sales in current year	$	$
Net sales in prior year		
(2) **Percentage change in net income:**		

a

a

a   **Corrected bank reconciliation for November:**
Balance per bank statement, Nov. 30
Add:

b   **Charm attempted to conceal the shortage by making the
following intentional errors in her reconciliation:**

c

a   *Accounts Receivable by Age Group*

	Amount	Percentage Considered Uncollectible	Estimated Uncollectible Accounts
Not yet due	$ 3 3 3 0 0 0		
1–30 days past due	1 3 5 0 0 0		
31–60 days past due	5 8 5 0 0		
61–90 days past due	1 3 5 0 0		
Over 90 days past due	2 2 5 0 0		
Totals	$ 5 6 2 5 0 0		

b   *General Journal*

a   *General Journal*

1996							
Var.*							

*The first three entries summarize entries occurring at various dates throughout the year.

b

NAGANO INTERNATIONAL
Aging of Accounts Receivable
Dec. 31, 19___

a

Customer	Total	Not Yet Due	1–30 Days Past Due	31–60 Days Past Due	61–90 Days Past Due	Over 90 Days Past Due
(418 names) Subtotals	$863125	$458975	$236700	$108350	$22500	$36600
J. Ardis						
N. Selstad						
Totals						

b

	Age Group Total	Percentage Considered Uncollectible	Estimated Uncollectible Accounts
Not yet due	$	1%	
1–30 days past due		4%	
31–60 days past due		10%	
61–90 days past due		30%	
Over 90 days past due		50%	
Totals			

c   *General Journal*

19__
Dec | **31**

d   **NAGANO INTERNATIONAL**
Partial Balance Sheet
Dec. 31, 19__

Current assets:

e   *General Journal*
19__
Jan | **7**

a   **Adolph Coors Company:**

    (1) **Accounts receivable turnover =**

a

Event	Current Assets	Liquidity (or Solvency)	Net Income	Net Cash Flow (from Any Source)
1				
2				
3				
4				
5				

b

1

					Cost	Current Market Value
a		Current assets:				
b						
Apr	10	Cash				
Aug	7	Cash				
c		Marketable Securities account:				
		Balance at Dec. 31, 1995				
d						
		Wolfe Computer, Inc. (4,000 shares; cost $50 per				
		Quality Foods				
e						
f						

g

a		General Journal						
19___								
Sept	**1**							

a

NAME _____

SECTION _____ DATE _____

a Perpetual inventory record card: FIFO basis

Item	CT-300	Inventory method	FIFO
Description	Cellular Telephone
Location	_____

Primary supplier _____

Secondary supplier _____

Inventory level: Minimum _____ Maximum _____

Date	PURCHASED Units	Unit Cost	Total	SOLD Units	Unit Cost	Cost of Goods Sold	BALANCE Units	Unit Cost	Balance
May 1							20	$40.00	$ 800.00
5				8					

b	General Journal						
19__							
May	5						

NAME _____

SECTION _____ DATE _____

a Perpetual inventory record card: LIFO basis

Item	DC-7	Inventory method	LIFO
Description		Desk chair	
Location			

Primary supplier	
Secondary supplier	
Inventory level: Minimum _____ Maximum _____	

	PURCHASED			SOLD			BALANCE		
Date	Units	Unit Cost	Total	Units	Unit Cost	Cost of Goods Sold	Units	Unit Cost	Balance
Sept 1							50	$60.00	$3,000.00
4	20	$65.00	$1,300.00				{ 50 20		

b	General Journal				
19___					
Sept	4				

a	General Journal					
1996						
	(1) Specific identification method:					
Jan 15	**Cost of Goods Sold**					
	Inventory					
	(2) Average-cost method:					
Jan 15						

California Irrigation (concluded)

b Inventory subsidiary ledger records:

(1) Specific identification method:

	PURCHASED			SOLD			BALANCE		
Date	Units	Unit Cost	Total	Units	Unit Cost	Cost of Goods Sold	Units	Unit Cost	Balance
Dec 12	600	$9.25	$5,550				600	$9.25	$ 5,550
Jan 9	900	9.50	8,550				{600 900	9.25 9.50}	14,100
Jan 15				}					

(2) Average-cost method:

	PURCHASED			SOLD			BALANCE		
Date	Units	Unit Cost	Total	Units	Unit Cost	Cost of Goods Sold	Units	Unit Cost	Balance
Dec 12	600	$9.25	$5,550				600	$9.25	$ 5,550
Jan 9	900	9.50	8,550				1,500	9.40*	14,100
Jan 15									

(3) First-in, first-out (FIFO) method:

	PURCHASED			SOLD			BALANCE		
Date	Units	Unit Cost	Total	Units	Unit Cost	Cost of Goods Sold	Units	Unit Cost	Balance
Dec 12	600	$9.25	$5,550				600	$9.25	$ 5,550
Jan 9	900	9.50	8,550				{600 900	9.25 9.50}	14,100
Jan 15				}					

(4) Last-in, first-out (LIFO) method:

	PURCHASED			SOLD			BALANCE		
Date	Units	Unit Cost	Total	Units	Unit Cost	Cost of Goods Sold	Units	Unit Cost	Balance
Dec 12	600	$9.25	$5,550				600	$9.25	$ 5,550
Jan 9	900	9.50	8,550				{600 900	9.25 9.50}	14,100
Jan 15				}					

a   **Cost of goods sold and ending inventory**

(1) **Average-cost method:**
    (a) **Cost of goods sold on July 28:**
          Average cost (as of July 22;
          Cost of goods sold

(2) **First-in, first-out (FIFO) method:**
    (a) **Cost of goods sold on July 28:**

(3) **Last-in, first-out (LIFO) method:**
    (a) **Cost of goods sold on July 28:**

b   **(1)**

a **Average-cost method:**

   Ending inventory at September 30:

   Average cost

   Cost of goods sold through September 30:

   Cost of goods available for sale

   Less:

b **First-in, first-out (FIFO) method:**

   Ending inventory at September 30:

   Cost of goods sold through September 30:

   Cost of goods available for sale

   Less:

c **Last-in, first-out (LIFO) method:**

   Ending inventory at September 30:

   Cost of goods sold:

a   Shrinkage loss—40 trees

(1)   Average-cost method:

(2)   Last-in, first-out (LIFO) method:

b   Shrinkage loss and LCM adjustment

(1)   Shrinkage loss, first-in, first-out (FIFO) method:

(2)   Write-down of inventory to the lower-of-cost-or-market:

	Units	Unit Cost	Total Cost
a Inventory and cost of goods sold:			
(1) FIFO:			
Inventory:			
Cost of goods sold:			
Cost of goods available for sale			
Less:			
(2) LIFO:			
Inventory:			
Cost of goods sold:			
(3) Average cost:			
Inventory:			
Cost of goods sold			

b

_____

_____

_____

_____

_____

_____

a   Cost of goods sold and ending inventory: perpetual inventory system

(1)   **Average cost method:**
    (a)   **Cost of goods sold on September 25:**
            Average cost as of September 23

    (b)   **Ending inventory at December 31:**

(2)   **First-in, first-out method (FIFO):**
    (a)   **Cost of goods sold on September 25:**

    (b)   **Ending inventory at December 31:**

(3)   **Last-in, first-out method (LIFO):**
    (a)   **Cost of goods sold on September 25:**

    (b)   **Ending inventory at December 31:**

b   **Ending inventory and cost of goods sold: periodic inventory system**

     (1)   **Average-cost method:**

         Ending inventory at December 31:

            Average cost ($

            Ending inventory

         Cost of goods sold:

            Cost of goods available for sale

            Less:

     (2)   **First-in, first-out (FIFO) method:**

     (3)   **Last-in, first-out (LIFO) method:**

c   **Entry to restate perpetual LIFO cost to periodic LIFO cost:**

d

a	1996	1995	1994
Net sales	$860000	$850000	$800000
Cost of goods sold			
Gross profit on sales			
Gross profit percentage			

a

(1) Estimating the cost of goods sold:

　　Cost ratio for the current year:

(2) Estimated ending inventory:

b

(1) Restating physical inventory from retail prices to cost:

　　Physical inventory stated in retail prices $70400

(2) Estimated shrinkage losses at cost:

c Computation of gross profit:

Net sales

Cost of goods sold:

a   Computations based on LIFO valuation of inventory:

   (1)   Inventory turnover rate:

   (2)   Current ratio:

   (3)   Gross profit rate:

b   Computations assuming that the company had used the FIFO
method of inventory valuation:

   (1)   Inventory turnover rate:

   (2)   Current ratio:

   (3)   Gross profit rate:

a

c   Expenditures that should be debited to the
Equipment account:

d   *General Journal*

19___

Dec | 31

a	Depreciation methods:	1 Straight-Line	2 MACRS
	Year		
	1995	$	$
	1996		
	1997		
	1998		
	1999		
	2000		
	Totals		
	(1) Straight-line computations:		
	1995: ($50,000 − $20,000) ×		
	1994–1999:		
	1999:		
	(2) MACRS computations:		

b _____

a Depreciation methods:	1 Straight-Line	2 MACRS
Year		
1994	$	$
1995		
1996		
1997		
1998		
1999		
Totals		
(1) Straight-line computations:		
1994: $80,000 ×		
1995–1998:		
1999:		
(2) MACRS computations:		
1994:		

b

a

| Year | Method of Depreciation | | |
	(1) Straight-Line	(2) 200%-Declining-Balance	(3) MACRS
1994	$	$	$
1995			
1996			
1997			
1998			
1999			
Totals			

Supporting Computations:

b

General Journal

19__					
Feb	10				

a

	Year		Depreciation in:	
			Financial Statements	Income Tax Returns
	1994 ($8,000 × ⅕ × ½); ($10,000 × 20%)		$ 800	$ 2000
	1995			
	1996			
	1997			
	1998			
	1999			
	Totals			

b

(1) Book value at Sept. 4, 1996:

    Cost

    Less:

(2) Gain or loss on disposal—financial statements:

c

(1) Tax basis at Sept. 4, 1996:

    Cost

    Less:

(2) Gain or loss on disposal for tax purposes:

d

General Journal

1996		
Sept	4	

a

	Year		Depreciation in: Financial Statements	Depreciation in: Income Tax Returns
	1994 ($16,000 × ⅛ × ³/₁₂); ($20,000 × 20%)		$	$
	1995			
	1996			
	1997			
	1998			
	1999			
	2000			
	2001			
	2002			
	Totals			

b

(1) Book value at March 19, 1996:

Cost

Less:

(2) Gain or loss on disposal—financial statements:

c

(1) Tax basis at March 19, 1996:

Cost

Less:

(2) Gain or loss on disposal for tax purposes:

d

General Journal

1996		
Mar	19	

a

a		**Cost of oil field less residual value (1)**					
		Estimated output (in barrels) (2)					
		Depletion rate per barrel					
		Adjusting Entries					
b							
1995							
Dec	31						
1996							
Dec	31						

a

Transaction	Current Ratio	Net Income	Taxable Income	Net Cash Flow (from All Sources)
1				
2				
3				
4				
5				
6				
7				
8				

b **1**

	Alpine Village	Nordic Sports
a Revised summary of balance sheet data:		
Assets		
Cash		
Accounts receivable (net of allowance for doubtful accounts)		
Inventory (LIFO basis)		
Plant and equipment:		
Land		
Building (net of accumulated depreciation)		
Equipment (net of accumulated depreciation)		
Total assets		
Liabilities & Stockholders' Equity		
Total liabilities		
Stockholders' equity *(4)*		
Total liabilities & stockholders' equity		

Supporting computations:

(1)

b   Revised cumulative net income:

	Alpine Village	Nordic Sports
Cumulative net income before adjustment	$	$
Adjustments for changes in accounting policies:		

c   Computation of the price that Scott is willing to pay for each business:

	Alpine Village	Nordic Sports
Computation of goodwill:		
Average annual net income (based on revisions in part **b**)		
Alpine:	$	
Nordic:		
Less: 20% return on revised stockholders' equity (part **a**)		
Alpine:		
Nordic:		
Earnings in excess of required return		

a

Transaction	Income Statement			Balance Sheet				
	Revenue	− Expenses	= Net Income	Assets	= Current Liabilities	+ Long-Term Liabilities	+ Owners' Equity	
a								
b								
c								
d								
e								
f								
g								
h								
i								
j								
k								
l								
*m								
*n								
*o								

*Supplemental Topic A, "Estimated Liabilities, Loss Contingencies, and Commitments."

a

GOOD 'N' LITE CANDY CO.
Partial Balance Sheet
December 31, 1995

Liabilities:
  Current liabilities:

  Long-term liabilities:

b   Comments on information in the numbered paragraphs:

   (1)

a		General Journal						
19___								
Aug	6							

b		Adjusting Entry						
Dec	31							

a and d

a

b		*General Journal*							
1995									
Oct	1								

c		*Amortization Table*						

(12%, 30-Year Mortgage Note Payable for $540,000; Payable in 360 Monthly Installments of $5,555)

Interest Period	Payment Date	Monthly Payment	Interest Expense	Reduction in Unpaid Balance	Unpaid Balance
Issue date	Sept. 1, 1995	—	—	—	$540000
1	Oct. 1	$5555	$5400	$155	539845
2	Nov. 1	5555	5398	157	539688
3					
4					

a

Amortization Table
(20% Note Payable for $15,215; Payable
in Four Semiannual Installments of $4,800)

Interest Period	Payment Date	Amount of Payment	Interest Expense	Reduction in Unpaid Balance	Unpaid Balance
Issue date	Dec. 31, 1995	—	—	—	$
1					
2					
3					
4					

b	General Journal					
1995						
Dec 31						
1996						
June 30						

General Journal

a						
1995						
Aug	1					
b						
Nov	1					
c						
Dec	31					
d						
1996						
May	1					

a   *General Journal*

	1996								
	May	1							

b   Balance sheet presentation of liabilities at
December 31, 1996:

Current liabilities:

Long-term liabilities:

c

a	General Journal		
(1)	**Bonds issued at 98:**		
1995			
Dec 31			
1996			
Mar			
(2)	**Bonds issued at 101:**		
1995			
Dec 31			
1996			
Mar			
b	Net bond liability at Dec. 31, 1996:	**Bonds Issued at 98**	**Bonds Issued at 101**

a

a

GULF COAST TELEPHONE COMPANY
Partial Balance Sheet
December 31, 1996

Liabilities:

  Current liabilities:

Long-term liabilities:

c **(1) Computation of debt ratio:**

  (2) Computation of interest coverage ratio:

b   (1)

	Coca-Cola	PepsiCo
a **Computation of ratios:**		
(1) **Return on assets:**		
Operating income (a)	$	$
Average total assets (b)	$	$
Return on assets [(a) ÷ (b)]	%	%
(2) **Return on equity:**		

b **(1)**

General Journal

a				LP		
Apr	7					

---

b	**DEAN ENGINEERING**		
	Statement of Owner's Capital		
	For the Month of April 19___		
Sharon Dean, capital, April 1, 19___			$
Add:			

a	SINCLAIR PRESS		
	Partial Balance Sheet		
	December 31, 1997		

Stockholders' equity

*Computation of retained earnings (or deficit) at December 31, 1997.

b   Note to financial statements:

a

BANNER PUBLICATIONS
Partial Balance Sheet
December 31, 1996

Stockholders' equity:

*Computation of retained earnings (or deficit) at December 31, 1996:

b **Note to financial statements:**

MANHATTAN TRANSPORT COMPANY
Partial Balance Sheet
December 31, 1997

Stockholders' equity:

*Computation of retained earnings or deficit at Dec. 31, 1997

Deficit at Dec. 31, 1995

Add:

a   *Bell Corporation*

Stockholders' equity:

b   *Parker Industries*

Stockholders' equity:

*Computation of retained earnings at Dec. 31, 1996:

(1) **DuPar Corporation**

a

b

(2) Irwin Products

a			General Journal								
1996											
Jan	**9**										
b											
1997											
June	**15**										

d

PACIFIC RIM CORPORATION
Partial Balance Sheet
December 31, 1997

Stockholders' equity:

*Computation of retained earnings (or deficit) at Dec. 31, 1997:
   Net income for 1996
   Less:

a	General Journal				
19___					
Jan	**6**				

b

MOBILE COMMUNICATIONS, INC.
Partial Balance Sheet
December 31, 19___

Stockholders' equity:

a　　　　　　*General Journal*

19___				
Apr	1			

b

PANCHO'S CANTINAS, INC.
Balance Sheet
April 30, 19___

Assets
Current assets:

Liabilities & Stockholders' Equity
Current liabilities:

a	Par value of all preferred stock outstanding				
	Par value per share of preferred stock				
	Number of shares of preferred stock outstanding				
b	Dividend requirement per share of preferred stock				
c					

a

GULF COAST AIRLINES
Income Statement
For the Year Ended December 31, 19___

Earnings per share of common stock:

b **Estimated net earnings per share next year:**

a

ACADEMIC TESTING SERVICES, INC.
Condensed Income Statement
For the Year Ended December 31, 1996

Earnings per share:

b

ACADEMIC TESTING SERVICES, INC.
Statement of Retained Earnings
For the Year Ended December 31, 1996

c

a

KELLER INTERIORS
Income Statement
For the Year Ended December 31, 1996

Earnings per share of capital stock:

b

KELLER INTERIORS
Statement of Retained Earnings
For the Year Ended December 31, 1996

Keller Interiors (concluded)

	Total Stockholders' Equity	Number of Shares Outstanding	Book Value per Share

NAME _____

SECTION _____ DATE _____

GRANITE HILLS CORPORATION
Statement of Stockholders' Equity
For the Year Ended December 31, 19___

Granite Hills Corporation

	Capital Stock ($10 Par Value)	Additional Paid-in Capital	Retained Earnings	Treasury Stock	Total Stockholders' Equity

a   *General Journal*

1996				

b

OVERNIGHT LETTER
Partial Balance Sheet
December 31, 1996

Stockholders' equity:

*Computation of retained earnings at Dec. 31, 1996:

c   Computation of maximum legal cash dividend per share at
Dec. 31, 1996:

a

b

a

MANDELLA CORPORATION
Partial Balance Sheet
December 31, 1995

b

MANDELLA CORPORATION
Partial Balance Sheet
December 31, 1996

Comprehensive Problem 7
Shadow Mountain Hotel

CHART OF ACCOUNTS

Balance Sheet Accounts		Income Statement Accounts	
Cash	101	Room rental revenue	400
Accounts receivable	105	Food & beverage sales	401
Allowance for doubtful accounts	106	Miscellaneous revenue	409
Stock subscriptions receivable	108		
Inventory (food & beverages)	110	Cost of goods sold	500
Supplies	112	Wages & salaries expense	502
Unexpired insurance	114	Advertising expense	504
		Water & utilities expense	506
Land	120	Uncollectible accounts expense	508
Buildings	122	Supplies expense	510
Accumulated depreciation: buildings	123	Insurance expense	512
Furniture & equipment	124	Depreciation expense: buildings	520
Accumulated depreciation: furniture & equipment	125	Depreciation expense: furniture & equipment	522
Goodwill	130	Amortization expense: intangible assets	528
Organization costs	132		
Accounts payable	201	Payroll taxes expense	540
Interest payable	205	Property taxes expense	542
Dividends payable: preferred stock	207	Income taxes expense	544
Unearned deposits	209	Interest expense	550
Income taxes withheld	221	Losses on disposal of plant assets	580
Social security taxes payable	222		
Medicare taxes payable	223	Gains on disposals of plant assets: (extraordinary)	600
Workers' compensation prem. payable	224		
SUTA taxes payable	225	Income summary	699
FUTA taxes payable	226		
Property taxes payable	227		
Income taxes payable	228		
Mortgage note payable	250		
Bonds payable	252		
Discount on bonds payable	253		
6% Cumulative preferred stock	300		
Common stock	310		
Common stock subscribed	311		
Stock dividend to be distributed	312		
Additional paid-in capital: common stock	320		
Additional paid-in capital: stock dividends	322		
Additional paid-in capital: treasury stock transactions	324		
Donated capital	330		
Retained earnings	340		
Treasury stock	350		
Dividends	360		

Page 1

General Journal

Date			LP		
1996					
June	3				

General Journal

Date				LP										
1996														

General Journal

Date		LP														
1996																

Page 4

General Journal

Date		LP				
1996						

General Journal

Date			LP		
1996					
	Adjusting Entries				
	(a)				

Page 6

General Journal

Date		LP										
1996												

General Journal

Date			LP											
1996		**Closing Entries**												

Inventory					Account No. 110
Date	Explanation	Ref	Debit	Credit	Balance
1996					
Var.	Summary of entries posted by staff	—	121300	118300	3000

Supplies					Account No. 112
Date	Explanation	Ref	Debit	Credit	Balance
1996					
Var.	Summary of entries posted by staff	—	71700		71700

Unexpired Insurance					Account No. 114
Date	Explanation	Ref	Debit	Credit	Balance
1996					
Var.	Summary of entries posted by staff	—	300000		300000

Land					Account No. 120
Date	Explanation	Ref	Debit	Credit	Balance
1996					

Buildings					Account No. 122
Date	Explanation	Ref	Debit	Credit	Balance
1996					

Cash — Account No. 101

Date	Explanation	Ref	Debit	Credit	Balance
1996					
Var.	Summary of entries posted by staff	—	2716600	1666360	1050240

Accounts Receivable — Account No. 105

Date	Explanation	Ref	Debit	Credit	Balance
1996					
Var.	Summary of entries posted by staff	—		48700	(48700)Cr.

Allowance for Doubtful Accounts — Account No. 106

Date	Explanation	Ref	Debit	Credit	Balance
1996					
Var.	Summary of entries posted by staff	—	48900		(48900)Dr.

Stock Subscriptions Receivable — Account No. 108

Date	Explanation	Ref	Debit	Credit	Balance
1996					

	Accumulated Depreciation: Buildings				Account No. 123
Date	Explanation	Ref	Debit	Credit	Balance
1996					

	Furniture & Equipment				Account No. 124
Date	Explanation	Ref	Debit	Credit	Balance
1996					

	Accumulated Depreciation: Furniture & Equipment				Account No. 125
Date	Explanation	Ref	Debit	Credit	Balance
1996					

	Goodwill				Account No. 130
Date	Explanation	Ref	Debit	Credit	Balance
1996					

	Organization Costs				Account No. 132
Date	Explanation	Ref	Debit	Credit	Balance
1996					

Accounts Payable					Account No. 201
Date	Explanation	Ref	Debit	Credit	Balance
1996					
Var.	Summary of entries posted by staff	—	117500	121300	3800

Interest Payable					Account No. 205
Date	Explanation	Ref	Debit	Credit	Balance
1996					
Var.	Summary of entries posted by staff	—	41000		(41000)Dr.

Dividends Payable: Preferred Stock					Account No. 207
Date	Explanation	Ref	Debit	Credit	Balance
1996					

Unearned Deposits					Account No. 209
Date	Explanation	Ref	Debit	Credit	Balance
1996					
Var.	Summary of entries posted by staff	—		381300	381300

Income Taxes Withheld					Account No. 221
Date	Explanation	Ref	Debit	Credit	Balance
1996					
Var.	Summary of entries posted by staff	—		86000	86000

Social Security Taxes Payable — Account No. 222

Date	Explanation	Ref	Debit	Credit	Balance
1996					
Var.	Summary of entries posted by staff	—		703 40	703 40

Medicare Taxes Payable — Account No. 223

Date	Explanation	Ref	Debit	Credit	Balance
1996					
Var.	Summary of entries posted by staff	—		181 40	181 40

Workers' Compensation Premiums Payable — Account No. 224

Date	Explanation	Ref	Debit	Credit	Balance
1996					
Var.	Summary of entries posted by staff	—		121 00	121 00

SUTA Taxes Payable — Account No. 225

Date	Explanation	Ref	Debit	Credit	Balance
1996					
Var.	Summary of entries posted by staff	—		97 20	97 20

FUTA Taxes Payable — Account No. 226

Date	Explanation	Ref	Debit	Credit	Balance
1996					
Var.	Summary of entries posted by staff	—		14 40	14 40

Property Taxes Payable — Account No. 227

Date	Explanation	Ref	Debit	Credit	Balance
1996					

Date	Explanation	Ref	Debit	Credit	Balance
	Income Taxes Payable				**Account No. 228**
1996					
Var.	Summary of entries posted by staff	—	3 0 5 0 0 0		(3 0 5 0 0 0)Dr.

Date	Explanation	Ref	Debit	Credit	Balance
	Mortgage Note Payable				**Account No. 250**
1996					

Date	Explanation	Ref	Debit	Credit	Balance
	Bonds Payable				**Account No. 252**
1996					

Date	Explanation	Ref	Debit	Credit	Balance
	Discount on Bonds Payable				**Account No. 253**
1996					

Date	Explanation	Ref	Debit	Credit	Balance
	6% Cumulative Preferred Stock				**Account No. 300**
1996					

Common Stock — Account No. 310

Date	Explanation	Ref	Debit	Credit	Balance
1996					

Common Stock Subscribed — Account No. 311

Date	Explanation	Ref	Debit	Credit	Balance
1996					

Stock Dividend to Be Distributed — Account No. 312

Date	Explanation	Ref	Debit	Credit	Balance
1996					

Additional Paid-in Capital: Common Stock — Account No. 320

Date	Explanation	Ref	Debit	Credit	Balance
1996					

Additional Paid-in Capital: Stock Dividends — Account No. 322

Date	Explanation	Ref	Debit	Credit	Balance
1996					

Additional Paid-in Capital: Treasury Stock Transactions Account No. 324

Date	Explanation	Ref	Debit	Credit	Balance
1996					

Donated Capital Account No. 330

Date	Explanation	Ref	Debit	Credit	Balance
1996					

Retained Earnings Account No. 340

Date	Explanation	Ref	Debit	Credit	Balance
1996					

Treasury Stock Account No. 350

Date	Explanation	Ref	Debit	Credit	Balance
1996					

Dividends Account No. 360

Date	Explanation	Ref	Debit	Credit	Balance
1996					

Room Rental Revenue — Account No. 400

Date	Explanation	Ref	Debit	Credit	Balance
1996					
Var.	Summary of entries posted by staff	—		1 9 7 9 1 00	1 9 7 9 1 00

Food & Beverage Sales — Account No. 401

Date	Explanation	Ref	Debit	Credit	Balance
1996					
Var.	Summary of entries posted by staff	—		3 2 2 3 00	3 2 2 3 00

Miscellaneous Revenue — Account No. 409

Date	Explanation	Ref	Debit	Credit	Balance
1996					
Var.	Summary of entries posted by staff	—		4 6 2 00	4 6 2 00

Cost of Goods Sold — Account No. 500

Date	Explanation	Ref	Debit	Credit	Balance
1996					
Var.	Summary of entries posted by staff	—	1 1 8 3 00		1 1 8 3 00

Wages & Salaries Expense — Account No. 502

Date	Explanation	Ref	Debit	Credit	Balance
1996					
Var.	Summary of entries posted by staff	—	6 0 5 0 00		6 0 5 0 00

Advertising Expense				Account No. 504	
Date	Explanation	Ref	Debit	Credit	Balance
1996					
Var.	Summary of entries posted by staff	—	30000		30000

Water & Utilities Expense				Account No. 506	
Date	Explanation	Ref	Debit	Credit	Balance
1996					
Var.	Summary of entries posted by staff	—	133500		133500

Uncollectible Accounts Expense				Account No. 508	
Date	Explanation	Ref	Debit	Credit	Balance
1996					

Supplies Expense				Account No. 510	
Date	Explanation	Ref	Debit	Credit	Balance
1996					

Insurance Expense				Account No. 512	
Date	Explanation	Ref	Debit	Credit	Balance
1996					

Depreciation Expense: Buildings — Account No. 520

Date	Explanation	Ref	Debit	Credit	Balance
1996					

Depreciation Expense: Furniture & Equipment — Account No. 522

Date	Explanation	Ref	Debit	Credit	Balance
1996					

Amortization Expense: Intangible Assets — Account No. 528

Date	Explanation	Ref	Debit	Credit	Balance
1996					

Payroll Taxes Expense — Account No. 540

Date	Explanation	Ref	Debit	Credit	Balance
1996					
Var.	Summary of entries posted by staff		67500		67500

Property Taxes Expense — Account No. 542

Date	Explanation	Ref	Debit	Credit	Balance
1996					

Income Taxes Expense — Account No. 544

Date	Explanation	Ref	Debit	Credit	Balance
1996					

Interest Expense — Account No. 550

Date	Explanation	Ref	Debit	Credit	Balance
1996					
Var.	Summary of entries posted by staff	—	205000		205000

Losses on Disposals of Plant Assets — Account No. 580

Date	Explanation	Ref	Debit	Credit	Balance
1996					

Gains on Disposals of Plant Assets (Extraordinary) — Account No. 600

Date	Explanation	Ref	Debit	Credit	Balance
1996					

Income Summary — Account No. 699

Date	Explanation	Ref	Debit	Credit	Balance
1996					

SHADOW MOUNTAIN CORPORATION
Income Statement
For the Three Months Ended September 30, 1996

Revenue:		
Room rental revenue		$
Food & beverage sales		
Miscellaneous revenue		
Total revenue		$
Expenses:		
Cost of goods sold	$	
Wages & salaries expense		
Advertising expense		
Water & utilities expense		
Uncollectible accounts expense		
Supplies expense		
Insurance expense		
Income before extraordinary items		$
Net income		$
Earnings per share of common stock:*		

SHADOW MOUNTAIN CORPORATION
Statement of Retained Earnings
For the Three Months Ended September 30, 1996

Retained earnings, July 1, 1996	$	–0–
Net income for the quarter ended September 30		
Subtotal		
Less:		

SHADOW MOUNTAIN CORPORATION
Balance Sheet
September 30, 1996

Assets			
Current assets:			
Cash			$
Accounts receivable		$	
Less:			
Plant and equipment:			
Land		$	
Buildings	$		
Less: Accumulated depreciation			
Furniture & equipment	$		
Less:			
Intangible assets:			
Goodwill		$	
Total assets			$

Liabilities & Stockholders' Equity			
Liabilities:			
Current liabilities:			
Accounts payable			$
Interest payable			
Long-term liabilities:			
Total liabilities			$
Stockholders' equity:			
6% Cumulative preferred stock, $100 par, 25,000 shares authorized and issued, 15,000 shares outstanding		$	
Total liabilities & stockholders' equity			$

SHADOW MOUNTAIN CORPORATION
After-Closing Trial Balance
September 30, 1996

Account	Debit	Credit
Cash	18 128 00	
Accounts receivable	46 2 00	
Allowance for doubtful accounts		9 00
Inventory	39 2 00	
Supplies	40 0 00	
Unexpired insurance		
Land		
Buildings		

a

a

EDUCATORS' OUTLET, INC.
Statement of Cash Flows
For the Year Ended December 31, 19___

Cash flows from operating activities:

Cash received from customers *(1)* .... $

Supporting computations:

(1) Cash received from customers:

a

FRANKLIN OPTICAL
Partial Statement of Cash Flows
For the Year Ended December 31, 19___

Cash flows from operating activities:

Supporting computations:

(1) Proceeds from sales of marketable securities:

(2) Proceeds from sales of plant assets:

b

Schedule of noncash investing and financing activities:

a

CARAVAN IMPORTS
Partial Statement of Cash Flows
For the Year Ended December 31, 19___

Cash flows from investing activities:

Supporting computations:

(1) Proceeds from sales of marketable securities:

(2) Proceeds from sales of plant assets:

b

Schedule of noncash investing and financing activities:

SATELLITE TRANSMISSIONS, INC.
Partial Statement of Cash Flows
For the Year Ended December 31, 19___

Cash flows from operating activities:

   Cash received from customers *(1)*

(1)   Cash received from customers:

(2)   Interest and dividends received:

SATELLITE TRANSMISSIONS, INC.
Partial Statement of Cash Flows
For the Year Ended December 31, 19___

Cash flows from operating activities:		
Net income		$203000
Add:	$	

CHILD'S PLAY, INC.
Partial Statement of Cash Flows
For the Year Ended December 31, 19___

Cash flows from operating activities:

   Cash received from customers *(1)* $

(1)   Cash received from customers:

(2)   Interest and dividends received:

(3)

CHILD'S PLAY, INC.
Partial Statement of Cash Flows
For the Year Ended December 31, 19___

Cash flows from operating activities:		
Net income		$190000
Add:	$	

INLAND WASTE MANAGEMENT, INC.

Statement of Cash Flows

For the Year Ended December 31, 19___

Cash flows from operating activities:

  Cash received from customers *(1)* $

  Interest received *(2)* $

Supporting computations:

(1) Cash received from customers:

(2) Interest received:

(3) **Cash paid to suppliers and employees:**

BARRAZA INDUSTRIES, INC.
Statement of Cash Flows
For the Year Ended December 31, 19___

Cash flows from operations:

    Cash received from customers (1) $

Supporting computations:

(1)   **Cash received from customers:**

(2)

(3) **Cash paid to suppliers and employees:**

a

ROADBUILDERS, INC.
Comparative Schedule of Profit Recognition (in millions)
Four-Year Forecast

b

Sales Journal

Date	Account Receivable Debited	Invoice no.	Terms	✓	Amount
19___					

General Journal

19___					

Purchases Journal
Page 5

Date	Account Payable Credited	Invoice Date	Terms	✓	Net Cost
19___					

General Journal
Page 5

		LP		

General Ledger

				Cash						Account No. 10	
Date		Explanation		Ref	Debit			Credit		Balance	
19___											

				Office Supplies						Account No. 18	
Date		Explanation		Ref	Debit			Credit		Balance	
19___											

				Land						Account No. 20	
Date		Explanation		Ref	Debit			Credit		Balance	
19___											

				Building						Account No. 22	
Date		Explanation		Ref	Debit			Credit		Balance	
19___											

				Notes Payable						Account No. 30	
Date		Explanation		Ref	Debit			Credit		Balance	
19___											

General Ledger

Accounts Payable				Account No. 32
Date	Explanation	Ref	Debit	Credit	Balance
19__					

Purchases				Account No. 60
Date	Explanation	Ref	Debit	Credit	Balance
19__					

Purchase Returns & Allowances				Account No. 62
Date	Explanation	Ref	Debit	Credit	Balance
19__					

Salaries Expense				Account No. 70
Date	Explanation	Ref	Debit	Credit	Balance
19__					

Purchase Discounts Lost				Account No. 80
Date	Explanation	Ref	Debit	Credit	Balance
19__					

Accounts Payable Subsidiary Ledger

American Products

Date	Explanation	Ref	Debit	Credit	Balance
19___					

King Corporation

Date	Explanation	Ref	Debit	Credit	Balance
19___					

Medco Labs

Date	Explanation	Ref	Debit	Credit	Balance
19___					

Ralston Company

Date	Explanation	Ref	Debit	Credit	Balance
19___					

Tricor Corporation

Date	Explanation	Ref	Debit	Credit	Balance
19___					

Accounts Payable Subsidiary Ledger

a | Vita-Life, Inc.

Date	Explanation	Ref	Debit	Credit	Balance
19___					

b

POISON CREEK DRUG STORE
Schedule of Accounts Payable
August 31, 19___

Comprehensive Problem 3
The Next Dimension: Part I

CHART OF GENERAL LEDGER ACCOUNTS

Account Title	Account Number	Account Title	Account Number
Cash	101	Income Summary	305
Notes Receivable	103	Sales	401
Accounts Receivable	104	Sales Returns and Allowances	402
Interest Receivable	106	Sales Discounts	404
Inventory	108	Cost of Goods Sold	501
Unexpired Insurance	110	Warehouse Wages Expense	601
Prepaid Advertising	112	Depreciation Expense:	
Supplies	113	Buildings	610
Land	120	Depreciation Expense:	
Buildings	122	Warehouse Equipment	611
Accumulated Depreciation:		Freight Expense	620
Buildings	123	Advertising Expense	622
Warehouse Equipment	130	Maintenance Expense	624
Accumulated Depreciation:		Utilities Expense	626
Warehouse Equipment	131	Supplies Expense	628
Office Equipment	132	Travel and Entertainment Expense	630
Accumulated Depreciation:		Inventory Shrinkage Losses	632
Office Equipment	133	Office Salaries Expense	701
Notes Payable	201	Depreciation Expense:	
Accounts Payable	205	Office Equipment	710
Salaries Payable	210	Insurance Expense	720
Interest Payable	212	Interest Revenue	801
Bailey Renner, Capital	301	Interest Expense	810
Bailey Renner, Drawing	303	Purchase Discounts Lost	812

		General Journal				Page 44
1996			LP			

General Journal

1996				LP			
		Adjusting Entries					

Page 46

General Journal

1996

LP

Adjusting Entries (continued)

General Journal (concluded)

1996				LP			
			Closing Entries				

Sales Journal and Purchases Journal

Sales Journal						Page 16
Date 1996	Accounts Receivable Debited	Invoice No.	A/R √	Invoice Amount	Inv. √	Cost of Goods Sold

Purchases Journal						Page 9
Date 1996	Accounts Payable Credited	Invoice Date	Terms	Inv. √	A/P √	Net Cost

Explanations of Events Not Requiring Journal Entries

Date	Description	Reason for Not Recording Item

General Ledger

		Cash					Account No. 101
Date	Explanation		Ref	Debit	Credit		Balance
1996							
May 31	Balance						1 5 6 2 3 0

		Notes Receivable					Account No. 103
Date	Explanation		Ref	Debit	Credit		Balance
1996							

		Accounts Receivable					Account No. 104
Date	Explanation		Ref	Debit	Credit		Balance
1996							
May 31	Balance						1 0 2 4 0 0

		Interest Receivable					Account No. 106
Date	Explanation		Ref	Debit	Credit		Balance
1996							

		Inventory					Account No. 108
Date	Explanation		Ref	Debit	Credit		Balance
1996							
May 31	Balance						9 2 7 7 0

General Ledger (continued)

Unexpired Insurance — Account No. 110

Date		Explanation	Ref	Debit	Credit	Balance
1996						
May	31	Balance				120

Prepaid Advertising — Account No. 112

Date		Explanation	Ref	Debit	Credit	Balance
1996						
May	31	Balance				2750

Supplies — Account No. 113

Date		Explanation	Ref	Debit	Credit	Balance
1996						
May	31	Balance				2800

Land — Account No. 120

Date		Explanation	Ref	Debit	Credit	Balance
1996						
May	31	Balance				370000

Buildings — Account No. 122

Date		Explanation	Ref	Debit	Credit	Balance
1996						
May	31	Balance				450000

General Ledger (continued)

Accumulated Depreciation: Buildings — Account No. 123

Date		Explanation	Ref	Debit	Credit	Balance
1996						
May	31	Balance				52500

Warehouse Equipment — Account No. 130

Date		Explanation	Ref	Debit	Credit	Balance
1996						
May	31	Balance				42000

Accumulated Depreciation: Warehouse Equipment — Account No. 131

Date		Explanation	Ref	Debit	Credit	Balance
1996						
May	31	Balance				19600

Office Equipment — Account No. 132

Date		Explanation	Ref	Debit	Credit	Balance
1996						
May	31	Balance				18000

General Ledger (continued)

Accumulated Depreciation: Office Equipment — Account No. 133

Date		Explanation	Ref	Debit	Credit	Balance
1996						
May	31	Balance				2100

Notes Payable — Account No. 201

Date		Explanation	Ref	Debit	Credit	Balance
1996						
May	31	Balance				300000

Accounts Payable — Account No. 205

Date		Explanation	Ref	Debit	Credit	Balance
1996						
May	31	Balance				301975

Salaries Payable — Account No. 210

Date		Explanation	Ref	Debit	Credit	Balance
1996						

Interest Payable — Account No. 212

Date		Explanation	Ref	Debit	Credit	Balance
1996						
May	31	Balance				750

General Ledger (continued)

Bailey Renner, Capital   **Account No. 301**

Date		Explanation	Ref	Debit	Credit	Balance
1996						
May	31	Balance				5 6 0 1 4 5

Bailey Renner, Drawing   **Account No. 303**

Date	Explanation	Ref	Debit	Credit	Balance
1996					

Income Summary   **Account No. 305**

Date	Explanation	Ref	Debit	Credit	Balance
1996					

Sales   **Account No. 401**

Date	Explanation	Ref	Debit	Credit	Balance
1996					

Sales Returns and Allowances   **Account No. 402**

Date	Explanation	Ref	Debit	Credit	Balance
1996					

General Ledger (continued)

Sales Discounts   Account No. 404

Date	Explanation	Ref	Debit	Credit	Balance
1996					

Cost of Goods Sold   Account No. 501

Date	Explanation	Ref	Debit	Credit	Balance
1996					

Warehouse Wages Expense   Account No. 601

Date	Explanation	Ref	Debit	Credit	Balance
1996					

Depreciation Expense: Buildings   Account No. 610

Date	Explanation	Ref	Debit	Credit	Balance
1996					

Depreciation Expense: Warehouse Equipment   Account No. 611

Date	Explanation	Ref	Debit	Credit	Balance
1996					

General Ledger (continued)

Freight Expense — Account No. 620

Date	Explanation	Ref	Debit	Credit	Balance
1996					

Advertising Expense — Account No. 622

Date	Explanation	Ref	Debit	Credit	Balance
1996					

Maintenance Expense — Account No. 624

Date	Explanation	Ref	Debit	Credit	Balance
1996					

Utilities Expense — Account No. 626

Date	Explanation	Ref	Debit	Credit	Balance
1996					

Supplies Expenses — Account No. 628

Date	Explanation	Ref	Debit	Credit	Balance
1996					

General Ledger (continued)

Travel and Entertainment Expense   Account No. 630

Date	Explanation	Ref	Debit	Credit	Balance
1996					

Inventory Shrinkage Losses   Account No. 632

Date	Explanation	Ref	Debit	Credit	Balance
1996					

Office Salaries Expense   Account No. 701

Date	Explanation	Ref	Debit	Credit	Balance
1996					

Depreciation Expense: Office Equipment   Account No. 710

Date	Explanation	Ref	Debit	Credit	Balance
1996					

Insurance Expense   Account No. 720

Date	Explanation	Ref	Debit	Credit	Balance
1996					

General Ledger (concluded)

	Interest Revenue					Account No. 801
Date	Explanation	Ref	Debit	Credit	Balance	
1996						

	Interest Expense					Account No. 810
Date	Explanation	Ref	Debit	Credit	Balance	
1996						

	Purchase Discounts Lost					Account No. 812
Date	Explanation	Ref	Debit	Credit	Balance	
1996						

Accounts Receivable Subsidiary Ledger

Atlantic Auto Supply

Date	Explanation	Ref	Debit	Credit	Balance
1996					
May 31	Balance				132 00

Electric City

Date	Explanation	Ref	Debit	Credit	Balance
1996					
May 31	Balance				178 00

POW Stereo

Date	Explanation	Ref	Debit	Credit	Balance
1996					
May 31	Balance				550 00

Stereo Depot

Date	Explanation	Ref	Debit	Credit	Balance
1996					
May 31	Balance				164 00

The Buzzer

Date	Explanation	Ref	Debit	Credit	Balance
1996					

Accounts Payable Subsidiary Ledger

Carnegie Acoustics

Date		Explanation	Ref	Debit	Credit	Balance
1996						
May	31	Balance				195000

Express Transport Co.

Date		Explanation	Ref	Debit	Credit	Balance
1996						
May	31	Balance				4075

Home Video, Inc.

Date		Explanation	Ref	Debit	Credit	Balance
1996						
May	31	Balance				102900

Comprehensive Problem 3
The Next Dimension: Part I (continued)

Inventory Subsidiary Ledger

| Item | Easy Rider Speaker Systems | Primary supplier | Carnegie Acoustics |
| Description | System for cars and trucks | Secondary supplier | None |

Date	PURCHASED			SOLD			BALANCE		
	Units	Unit Cost	Total	Units	Unit Cost	Total	Units	Unit Cost	Balance
May 31							500	$68	$34,000

Comprehensive Problem 3
The Next Dimension: Part I (continued)

Inventory Subsidiary Ledger (continued)

Item	MegaMite Speaker Systems	Primary supplier	Carnegie Acoustics
Description	Speakers for homes and offices	Secondary supplier	None

Date	PURCHASED			SOLD			BALANCE		
	Units	Unit Cost	Total	Units	Unit Cost	Total	Units	Unit Cost	Balance
May 31							300	$93	$27,900

Comprehensive Problem 3
The Next Dimension: Part I (continued)

Inventory Subsidiary Ledger (concluded)

Item _____SuperScreen TVs_____

Description _____42" high definition television sets_____

Primary supplier _____Home Video, Inc._____

Secondary supplier _____None_____

Date	PURCHASED				SOLD				BALANCE		
	Units	Unit Cost	Total		Units	Unit Cost	Total		Units	Unit Cost	Balance
May 31									30	$1,029	$30,870

Explanations of Adjustments on the Worksheet

Explanations of adjustments:

a Insurance expired during June: $120 + ($3600 \div 12 \times \frac{1}{2}) = $270.

b

THE NEXT DIMENSION
Income Statement
For the Month Ended June 30, 1996

Gross sales				$
Sales returns & allowances		$		
Sales discounts				
Net sales				$
Less: Cost of goods sold				
Gross profit				$
Less: Operating expenses:				
Selling expenses:				
Warehouse wages expense	$			
Depreciation expense: buildings				

THE NEXT DIMENSION
Statement of Owner's Equity
For the Month Ended June 30, 1996

Bailey Renner, Capital, May 31, 1996		$
Add:	$	

THE NEXT DIMENSION			
Balance Sheet (and Note to Accompany Financial Statements)			
June 30, 1996			
Assets			
Current assets:			
Cash			$
Notes receivable			
Accounts receivable			
Interest receivable			
Plant and equipment:			
Land		$	
Buildings	$		
Less:			
Total assets			
Liabilities & Owner's Equity			
Current liabilities:			
			$
Long-term liabilities:			

Note to Accompany Financial Statements:

Note 1: Contingencies

THE NEXT DIMENSION
Schedule of Accounts Receivable
June 30, 1996

Atlantic Auto Supply		$

THE NEXT DIMENSION
Schedule of Accounts Payable
June 30, 1996

Carnegie Acoustics		$

THE NEXT DIMENSION
Schedule of Inventory
June 30, 1996

Type of Product	Quantity	Unit Cost	Total Cost

THE NEXT DIMENSION
After-Closing Trial Balance
June 30, 1996

Cash	$	
Notes receivable		
Accounts receivable		
Interest receivable		
Inventory		
Unexpired insurance		
Prepaid advertising		
Supplies		
Land		
Buildings		
Accumulated depreciation: buildings		$
Warehouse equipment		
Accumulated depreciation: warehouse equipment		
Office equipment		
Accumulated depreciation: office equipment		
Notes payable		

a $15,000 ×

a	Present value of future principal payment:		
	$50,000,000 due after 20 semiannual periods,		
	discontinued at 5% per period: $50,000,000 ×		
b	*General Journal*		
June 30			

a		**Present value of 24 monthly payments of $1,200 each, discounted at 1½% per month**				
b						
Dec	1					
c		**Current liabilities:**				
		Notes payable *(1)*				$
		(1)				

		General Journal															
a		Entries to record capital lease transactions in															
		lessor's accounting records:															
1996																	
(1)																	
Nov	1	Lease Payments Receivable (net)															
		Cost of Goods Sold					1 8 1 2 0										
(2)																	
	30	Cash															
		Interest Revenue															
		Lease Payments Receivable															
		To record receipt of first monthly payment from Star															
		Industries and to recognize finance charges earned in															
		month															
(3)																	
Dec	31																
b		Entries to record capital lease transactions in															
		lessee's accounting records:															
1996																	
(1)																	
Nov	1	Leased Equipment															

General Journal

1996					
(2)					
Nov	30	Interest Expense			
		Lease Payment Obligation			
		Cash			
		To record first monthly lease payment to Beach			
		Equipment Co. and to recognize one month's interest			
		charge on unpaid balance of lease payment obligation			
(3)					
Dec	31				
(4)					
	31				
c		Computation of net carrying value of leased equipment			
		at Dec. 31, 1996:			
		Leased equipment			
		Less:			
d		Computation of lease payment obligation at			
		Dec. 31, 1996:			
		Lease payment obligation, Nov. 1, 1996			$
		Less: Portions of monthly payments applied to principal;			
		November payment		$	
		December payment			
		Lease payment obligation, Dec. 31, 1996			

		Present value of payments under five-year lease:					
a		Present value of payments under five-year lease:					
		Down payment					
		Present value of $1,000,000 annually for five years, discounted at 10%					
		Present value of $3,000,000 due in five years, discounted at 10%					
		Total					
		Present value of payments under 10-year lease:					
b							

a

	Column			
Case	Type of Credit Transaction 1	Currency Used in Contract 2	Exchange Rate Direction 3	Effect on Income 4
a				

a		*General Journal*				
19__						
b		**Computation of exchange rate on Jan. 11:**				

c _____

_____

_____

_____

_____

_____

_____

_____

a		*General Journal*					
19__							

b		*Adjusting Entry*					
Dec	31						

D–5
Wolfe Computer

a		General Journal												
19__														
Oct	**28**													

		General Journal			
b		**Adjusting Entries**			
Dec	31				
c		**Computation of unit sales price:**			
d		**Computation of exchange rate for yen on Nov. 27:**			

e

a   **Compute gross income:**
    Total income
    Deduct:

b   **Compute adjusted gross income:**
    Gross income (per *a* above)
    Less:

c   **Compute taxable income:**

d   **Compute amount of tax remaining to be paid:**
    Taxable income (see *c* above)
    Tax on first $

a

Joint return for Mike and Peggy Stevens

Gross income:

b

Computation of tax liability and tax due (or refund)

Taxable income excluding long-term capital gain:

a Determination of taxable income on revised basis:			
Income before income taxes (before revision)			$250000
Less:			

		Before Accounting Changes	After Accounting Changes
b Tax reduction resulting from accounting changes:			
Tax on first $		$	$
Tax on next $			

NAME _____

SECTION _____ DATE _____

a	RUGER CORPORATION Income Statement For the Year Ended December 31, 1996		
Net sales			$7 500 000
Cost of goods sold			5 400 000
Gross profit on sales			$
Operating expenses:			
Selling expenses		$ 720 000	
Administrative expenses		780 000	
Total operating expenses			
Income before income taxes			$

Schedule A, Income Tax Computation:

b Journal entry at December 31, 1996:

c Journal entry at December 31, 1997:

	1997	1996

a Net sales:

d

CUSTOM LOGOS, INC.
Condensed Comparative Income Statement
For the Years Ended December 31, 1997 and December 31, 1996

	1997	1996
Net sales	$	$
Cost of goods sold		
Gross profit		
Operating expenses		
Income before income taxes		
Income taxes expense		
Net income		

e   **Favorable and unfavorable trends:**

a   Common size income statement:

	Sub Zero, Inc.	Industry Average
Sales (net)	100 %	100 %
Cost of goods sold		57
Gross profit on sales		43 %
Operating expenses:		
Selling		16 %
General and administrative		20
Total operating expenses		36 %
Operating income		7 %
Income taxes		3
Net income		4 %

b

a

(1) Inventory turnover:

(2) Accounts receivable turnover:

b

a

(1) Inventory turnover:

(2) Accounts receivable turnover:

b

a	Another World	Imports, Inc.
(1) Working capital:		
(2) Current ratio:		

b

a **Computation of quick assets, current assets, and current liabilities at the beginning of the year:**

Quick assets:

Current assets:

c **Effect of transactions:**

Item	Current Ratio	Quick Ratio	Working Capital	Net Cash Flow from Operating Activities
				Effect on
(0) Sold inventory on account at a loss				
(1) Issued capital stock for cash				
(2) Sold temporary investments at a loss				
(3) Acquired temporary investments				
(4) Wrote off uncollectible accounts				
(5) Sold inventory on account at a gain				
(6) Acquired plant and equipment for cash ...				
(7) Declared a cash dividend				
(8) Declared a 10% stock dividend				
(9) Paid accounts payable				
(10) Purchased goods on account				
(11) Collected cash on accounts receivable ...				
(12) Borrowed cash on a short-term note				

(1)